i was born in

manhattan

C000047894

don't make tee shirts that say "manhattan." it's always "brooklyn." yeah, right! i say the hell with it. why pretend to be down to earth?

I feel sorry for people who come to new york and don't know anybody who lives here who could show them around.

manhattan is still what we think of when we say "new york."

i see them hanging around midtown, which is very **boring,** although that tour of radio city is pretty cool.

and you know it!

I WANT TO TAKE THEM TO THE PLACES I REALLY love IN MY CITY.

THIS BOOK IS THE CLOSEST I COULD GET. a hundred guide books have ten thousand new york shops and restaurants. especially restaurants.

HOW CAN ANYBODY POSSIBLY TELL

?

and those

HIP

GUIDES are even worse.

all those TRENDY

design-y places,

all over the **world,** look just alike and attract the very SAME CROWD.

you know, the museum cafe type.

i mean, WHY TRAVEL?

it's more fun to mix it up: GENERIC places and cheap places and fancy traditional ones and hip ones and just plain silly ones.

i once saw a poster from the 20s that said, "I HAVE FORGOTTEN TO FORGET-TOOTS PAKA." i have no idea what it was about but i have forgotten to forget it. i keep a list of everything i've forgotten to forget, plus addresses, telephone numbers and random thoughts that connect together in a right-brain, non-linear way. i categorize friends and keep track of appointments without using alphabetical order or page numbers, which explains a lot. i go by how the pages look: the doodles and variations in handwriting. i thought other people might want to draw and write in a book with stuff already in it. a white page is so scary! so i left out a few things to make room. as of today, my list is 489 pages long. i also keep doodles my father robert drew in 1967, tickets and labels of all kinds, postcards of kittens dressed as rabbis, and the new york times obituary of georges de mestral, the man who invented velcro. (what a sad day!)

NEW YORK

NotEbook

smushing IS AN INEVITABLE

TOGETHER

this book is manhattan-**centric** and **downtown** slanted, because that's what i know about.

the NEW YORK-iest ones.

it isn't an accurate, fair, comprehensive guide at all. **it's personal.**

of a lifetime of living in new york plus juicy bits from these lists and different pieces of garbage i found particularly attractive. i hope you dig it. and if anybody knows anything about toots paka, please contact me at the earliest opportunity.

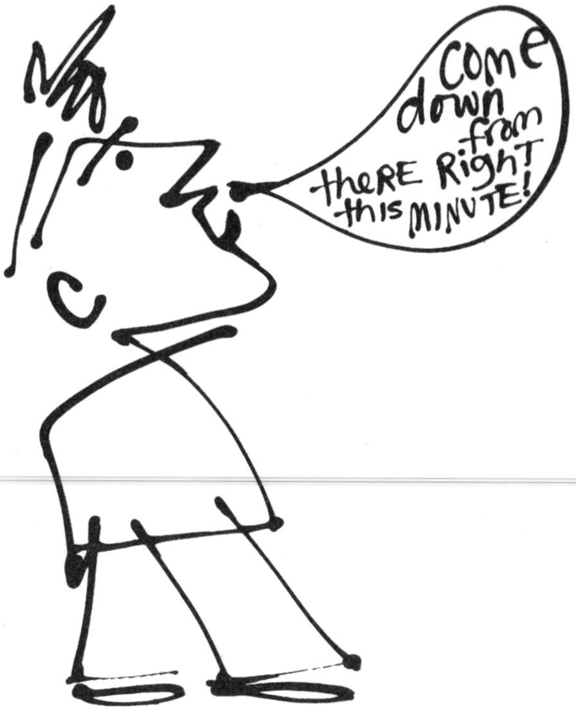
come down from there Right this MINUTE!

new york

notebook

by laurie rosenwald

CHRONICLE BOOKS

SAN FRANCISCO

all phone numbers are 212 unless they're not.

THIS IS MY BOOK:

iNg☆

nice small *friendly*

(even though they're hipster)

hotels

larchmont hotel
27 w. 11th st.
989 9333

incentra village house
32 8th ave.
206 0007

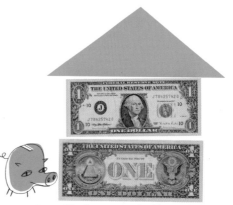

it's **unbelievably** CHEAP:
seafarers and international house
123 e. 15th st. 677 4800
res@sihnyc.org

RICE and BEANS

LA

874-2780

CARIDAD

2199 Broadway at 78th St.

one day i called the **WORLD**

253 w.125 st.
749 5838

RAINBOW MUSIC IS THE PLACE TO GO 102 WEST 125 ST. FOR THE SOULFUL AND THE SPIRITUAL ALSO THOSE FLYERS THAT TELL YOU GOOD WHERE THE

GOSP

FAMOUS 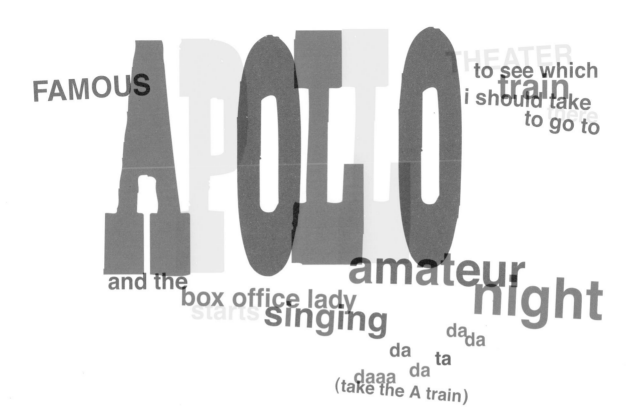 APOLLO THEATER

to see which
train
i should take
there
to go to

and the
box office lady
starts singing
amateur
night

da da
da ta
da
daaa da
(take the A train)

favorite harlem spot
the jamaican hot pot
2260 7th ave.
at west 133rd st.
491 5270

 SERVICES
ARE HAPPENING

I'VE MADE SOME REALLY FASCINATING MISTAKES HERE, AND SO CAN YOU!

ALL KINDS OF MIU MIU, CLERGERIE, THE NUTTIEST STYLES. **ANBAR SHOES   60 READE ST.   227 0253**

ORSO RESTAURANT 322 w. 46 st. 489 7212 is the only after theater place about which i can use the phrase "after theater" without gagging. it's truly italian, especially the liver. reservation, reservation, reservation.

2ND ACTING blend in with the smokers at intermush of a broadway show, about 9:30, go back in with them, hang back + wait until they're seated and grab an empty.

PLAYBILL

AN PLAYBILL LLEGAL THING 2 DO JUST

1CE

.ikea

from port authority

call 1 800 BUSIKEA
to go to the
elizabeth, n.j. store

CAFE WHA? PORTO RICO IMPORTING CO
201 BLEECKER ST   477 5421 or 1 800 453 5908
it's bred in the bean.

No matter what your interest, it will, nay, *must*, be satisfied by one of the luminaries speaking at the beautiful beaux-arts celeste bartos forum. the new york public library's public programs feature the likes of martin amis reading his latest in the fanciest, schmanciest room in the city. to order tickets, call 930 0571. thought provoking! harold bloom and jose saramago? well, whyever not? you could do a lot worse.

ROSENWORLD'S MINI MODERNISM TOUR
The International Style. Boring, but in a really great way.

Tishman   1957
666 Fifth Ave.
Architects: Carson & Lundin

United Nations Headquarters   1952
United Nations Plaza
43rd St. and the East River
Architect: Le Corbusier

Lever House   1952
390 Park Ave. near 54th St.
Architects: Skidmore, Owings, and Merrill

Seagram   1958
375 Park Ave.
Have a drink, or at least check out
the ladies room at The Four Seasons Restaurant.
The entrance is at 99 East 52 St.
Architects: Mies van der Rohe, Philip Johnson

SERVICE

ALLSTATE 333 3333

SAFEWAY 718 336 1010

CARMEL 666 6666

because nothing
says "i love you"
like  **meat**

serving all your rabbit,
buffalo, venison, and ostrich
needs since 1900.
reserve your thanksgiving
alligator now!

ottomanelli
285 bleecker st.
675 4217

where are the cute guys?

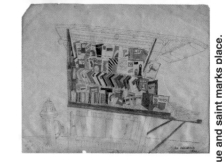

playing pool at sophies bar! 509 e. 5th st.   228 5680

EGG CREAM!

no eggs. no cream. you know, an egg cream!

FOX'S
u-bet
CHOCOLATE
FLAVOR SYRUP

*at www.foodlocker.com

for 2 servings

2 cups milk
1/2 cup seltzer
 (from a pressurized bottle)
1/4 cup Fox's U-Bet Syrup*

pour 1 cup of milk into a 12-ounce glass.
top with a spritz of seltzer so
that the white foam reaches the top
of the glass. place a spoon
in the glass. pour 2 tablespoons
of the chocolate syrup into the glass,
hitting the bottom of the spoon if possible,
and stir with quick strokes to blend the
syrup into the milk without deflating the foam.
repeat to make another egg cream.
serve immediately.

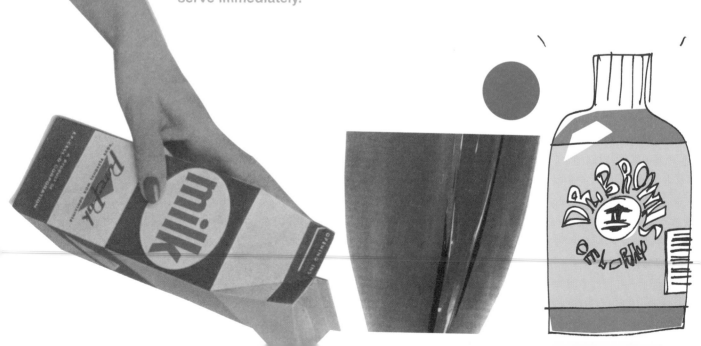

how to make
a superior manhattan:

3/4 oz sweet vermouth
2 1/2 oz blended bourbon
dash angostura bitters
2 or 3 ice cubes
1 maraschino cherry
1 twist of orange peel

combine the vermouth, whiskey,
bitters, and ice in a mixing
glass. stir gently. place the
cherry in a chilled cocktail glass
and strain the whiskey mixture
over the cherry. rub
the cut edge of the orange
peel over the rim of
the glass and twist it
over the drink to
release the oils but
don't drop it in.

MANHATTAN!

CEL-RAY!

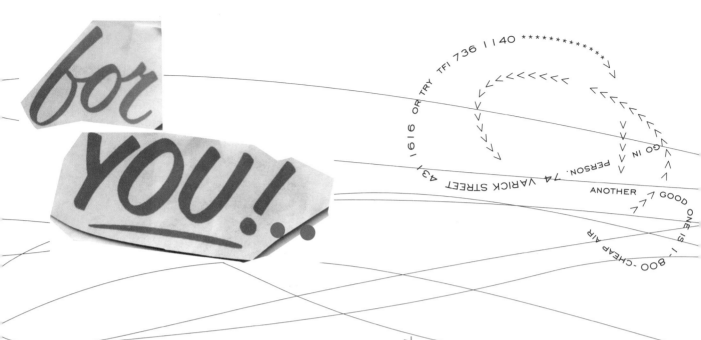

for
YOU!

OR TRY TFI 736 1140 ************
<<<<<<<
GO IN
PERSON. 74 VARICK STREET 431 1616
ANOTHER GOOD ONE IS 1-800-CHEAP AIR

MUSEUMS

PAY WHATEVER YOU WANT

American Museum of Natural History
The Brooklyn Childrens Museum
The Brooklyn Museum of Art
The Cloisters
Dia Center for the Arts
Isamu Noguchi Garden Museum
El Museo del Barrio
Metropolitan Museum of Art
The Museum of the City of New York
New York City Fire Museum
New York Historical Society
P.S. 1 Contemporary Art Center
Pierpont Morgan Library
Queens Museum of Art
Seaman's Church Institute
Staten Island Institute of Arts & Sciences

FREE FREE FREE ALL THE TIME

Artists' Space
American Numismatic Society
Asia Society (from noon to 2pm weekdays)
Carnegie Hall/Rose Museum
Dahesh Museum
The Drawing Center
Franklin Furnace
Goethe House German Cultural Center
Guggenheim Museum Soho
The Hispanic Society of America
The Municipal Art Society
Museum of American Folk Art
National Museum of the American Indian
New York City Police Museum
Snug Harbor Cultural Center
Taipei Gallery
Whitney Museum at Philip Morris

FREE DAYS + PAY WHATEVER DAYS

Tuesdays
Brooklyn Botanic Garden (all day)
Cooper-Hewitt (from 5-9pm)
Jewish Museum (from 5-8pm)
Wave Hill (all day)

Wednesdays
Bronx Museum of the Arts (all day)
Childrens Museum of the Arts
(from 5-7pm)

Thursdays
American Craft Museum
(from 6-8pm)
New Museum of Contemporary Art
(from 6-8pm)

Fridays
ICP (from 6-8pm)
MOMA (from 4-8:15 pm)
Guggenheim (from 6-8pm)
Whitney Museum (from 6-9pm)

Saturdays
Brooklyn Botanic Garden
(from 10am-noon)
Studio Museum in Harlem (first Sat.
of each month)

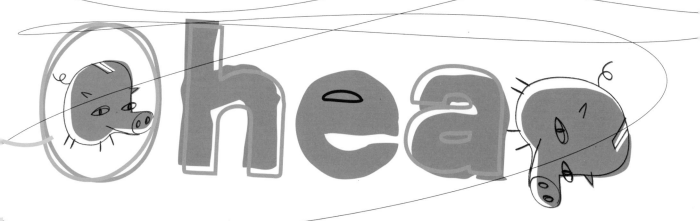

..... NOW VOYAGER IS THE DIRT CHEAP

ON SPECIAL... IT'S EASIER JUST

JUST CALL AND GO GO GO WHEREVER THEY'VE GOT

and here's one cheap and perfect
japanese restaurant. that's rare!
especially if you like alligator. NATORI
58 st. mark's place   533 7711

burgers, fries. great neighborhood hangout.

In this business you either sink or swim or you don't.
-David Snell

so you think you're a
COMEDIAN?

stephen rosenfield teaches comedy classes:
247 5555 comedyinstitute.com

you know, **NORMAL.** CORNER BISTRO 331 w. 4th st. 242 9502

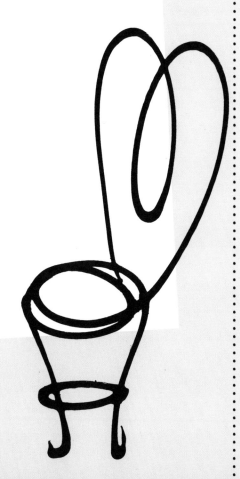

it's never too late to make a fool of yourself.

COP
bars and hangouts

meet good cops and bad cops!

(the d.a. told me
when i was on jury duty)

nearys pub
358 east 57 street   751 1434

wicked wolf restaurant
1442 1st avenue   861 4670

the last old-fashioned male strip joint is on 46th street

you know what? i love men. both
in and out of uniform.

THE GAIETY

and broadway above the howard johnson's. do they still have those fried clams? i mean at hojo's.

FIND YOUR INNER SWEDE!

H55 17 little west 12th st. 462 4559

make some JANSSONS FRESTELSE
(jansson's temptation)

Peel and slice the potatoes thinly. Slice the onions thinly. Butter a casserole, about 9x12 inches. Alternate layers of the potatoes, onions, and anchovies in the dish, starting with potatoes. Make several layers, dotting with butter all the time. Put the breadcrumbs and pepper on top, and bake in a 400° oven for 30 minutes. Then take it out and pour in cream around the edges, so you don't "wake up" the breadcrumbs. Bake another 20 minutes. Make sure the potatoes are really done! It's good with with rye bread, salad, and beer.

5-6 medium potatoes
2 large yellow onions
15-20 anchovy fillets
2 T butter
3/4 C heavy cream
bread crumbs
freshly ground black pepper

AQUAVIT restaurant
13 W. 54th St.
307 7311
try:
anything with
löjrom (bleak roe)
flavored aquavit
skål!
really really great

movies, design, and nordic kultur at
Scandinavia House
58 Park Avenue
(between 37th & 38th Streets)
779 3587
info@amscan.org

"does this sword make me look fat?"

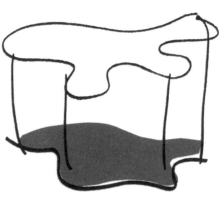

sells the scandinaviest bäst furniture and lamps and ceramics from the '50s and '60s

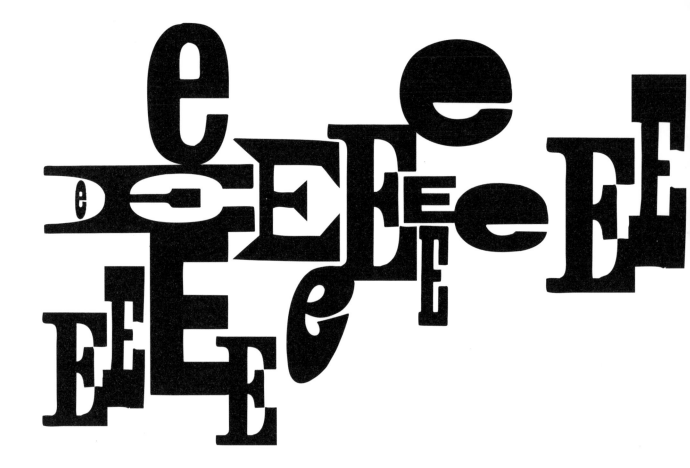

THE **E** TRAIN IS MY FAVORITE TRAIN BECAUSE IT SNAKES ALL OVER THE CITY

in AN **UNEXPECTED** WAY

FROM WAY DOWNTOWN TO **THE PARK** AND THEN DEEPEST QUEENS.

When this hash house shuts
down I'm On Wheels, sugar.
I'm gonna 86 this town
if there's no more
EISENBERG'S SANDWICH SHOP
174 Fifth Ave. 675-5096
Since 1929 my favorite
greasy spoon's been makin'
egg creams, wearin' hairnets,
and yellin' "Whiskey Down"
(rye bread) to whoever will listen.
The ultimate tuna salad, a
classic breakfast special.

And make sure to visit
Phil's Hawaiian Room.

Adam and Eve on a raft: Two poached eggs on toast.
Adam's ale: Plain water.
Axle grease or Skid grease: Butter.
Moo juice, sweet Alice or cow juice: Milk.
Belch water: Seltzer or soda water.
Birdseed: Cereal.
Blue-plate special: A dish of meat, potato,
and vegetable served on a plate (usually blue)
sectioned in three parts.
Bossy in a bowl: Beef stew, so called because "Bossy"
was a common name for a cow.
Bowl of red: A bowl of chili con carne, so called
for its deep red color.
Bowwow: A hot dog.
Breath: Onion.
Bridge or bridge party:
Four of anything, so called from the card-game hand of bridge.
Bullets: Baked beans,
also called "whistle berries" or "Saturday nights"
so called because of the supposed flatulence they cause.
Bun pup: A hot dog.
Burn one: Put a hamburger on the grill.
Burn the British: A toasted English muffin.
Cat's eyes or fish eyes: Tapioca
China: Rice pudding.
Chopper: A table knife.
City juice: Water.
Clean up the kitchen: Hash or hamburger.
Coney Island chicken or Coney Island:
A hot dog, so called because hot dogs
were popularly associated with the
Coney Island stands at which they were sold
Cowboy: A western omelet or sandwich
Cow feed: A salad.
Creep: Draft beer.
Crowd: Three of anything (possibly from the old saying,
"Two's company, three's a crowd").
Deadeye: Poached egg.
Dog and maggot: Cracker and cheese.
Dog biscuit: Cracker.
Dog's body: A pudding of pea soup and flour or hardtack.
Dough well done with cow to cover: Buttered toast.
Draw one: Coffee.
Eighty-six: "Do not sell to that customer" or "The kitchen is out of
the item ordered." Perhaps from the practice at Chumley's Restaurant
in New York City of throwing rowdy customers out the back
door, which is No.86 Bedford Street.

Eve with a lid on: Apple pie, referring to the
biblical Eve's tempting apple and to the crust that covers it.
Fifty-five: A glass of root beer.
First lady: Spareribs, a pun on Eve's being made from Adam's rib.
Fly cake or roach cake: A raisin cake or huckleberry pie.
Frenchman's delight: Pea soup.
GAC: Grilled American cheese sandwich.
Gentleman will take a chance: Hash.
Go for a walk: An order to be packed and taken out.
Gravel train: Sugar bowl.
Graveyard stew: Milk toast.
Groundhog: Hot dog.
Hemorrhage: Ketchup.
High and dry: A plain sandwich without butter or mayonnaise.
Houseboat: A banana split made with ice cream and sliced bananas.
In the alley: Serve as a side dish.
Irish turkey: Corned beef and cabbage.
Java or Joe: Coffee.
Looseners: Prunes, so called because of their laxative effect.
Lumber: A toothpick.
Maiden's delight: Cherries, so called because "cherry"
is a slang term for the maidenhead.
Mike and Ike or the twins: Salt and pepper shakers.
Mud or Omurk: Black coffee.
Murphy: Potatoes, so called because of their association with
the Irish diet of potatoes, Murphy being a common Irish name.
Noah's boy: A slice of ham, because Ham was Noah's second son.
No cow: Without milk.
On the hoof: Meat done rare.
On wheels: An order to be packed and taken out.
Pair of drawers: Two cups of coffee.
Pittsburgh: Toast or something burning, so called because of the
smokestacks evident in Pittsburgh, a coal-producing and
steel-mill city. In meat cookery, this refers to a piece of meat
charred on the outside while still red within.
Put out the lights and cry: Liver and onions.
Radio: A tuna-fish-salad sandwich on toast punning on "tuna down"
which sounds like "turn it down," as one would the radio knob.
Sand: Sugar.
Sea dust: Salt.
Sinkers and suds: Doughnuts and coffee.
Vermont: Maple syrup, because maple syrup comes from Vermont.
Warts: Olives.
Wreath: Cabbage.
Wreck 'em: Scramble the eggs.
Yum-yum: Sugar.
Zeppelins in a fog: Sausages in mashed potatoes.

pepe

picolissimo place with perfect italian food

and even picolissimo-er prices.

pellegrino limonata too. and they deliver.

149 sullivan street 677 4555.

ITS A PARTY!

THROW YOUR COAT RIGHT ON THAT BED! OLDER WOMEN! YOUNGER MEN! MAKE A DEAL! HAVE A BABY! COME DANCE ON OUR DEEP PILE CARPETS! HOW ABOUT SOME THAI MEAT LOLLIPOPS? WITH SPECIAL GUESTS BRITNEY SPEARS, DONATELLA VERSACE, ELTON JOHN, JENNIFER LOPEZ, NOAM CHOMSKY, PAMELA ANDERSON, STING, OPRAH, PRINCE, AND MADONNA!

MAGIC NUMBER FOR A SMALL PARTY: 11.

DIAMOND ICE CUBE CO DELIVERS. 675 4115

grand brass

is a paradise of lamp parts + hardware
221 grand st.   226 2567

notes

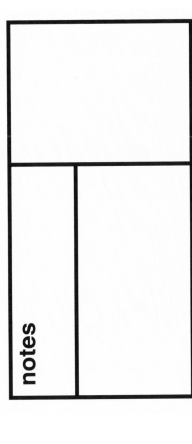

blather, hyperbole, claptrap.

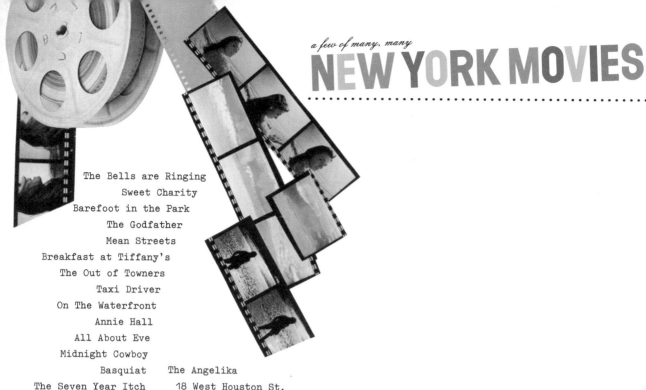

The Bells are Ringing
Sweet Charity
Barefoot in the Park
The Godfather
Mean Streets
Breakfast at Tiffany's
The Out of Towners
Taxi Driver
On The Waterfront
Annie Hall
All About Eve
Midnight Cowboy
Basquiat
The Seven Year Itch
Tootsie
The Producers
GoodFellas
West Side Story
A Bronx Tale
Rear Window

The Angelika
18 West Houston St.
995 2000
Film Forum
209 West Houston St.
727 8110
Lincoln Plaza
Broadway between
62nd and 63rd St.
757 2280
Walter Reade Theater
70 Lincoln Center
Plaza
875 5600

ALWAYS

A GOOD MOVIE AT: ▶

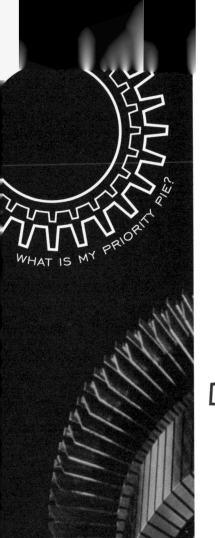

WHAT IS MY PRIORITY PIE?

PETS

SHELTER

CLOTHING

FOOD

EXQUISITE PLANTS AND FLOWERS   Takashimaya   693 Fifth Avenue   350 0100

how to feel rich: buy a 40 dollar metro card

FIND
A L C O N E
WEST   NYC,   AT   235
633 0551. ARE YOU   FRESH   OUT   OF
CLOWNDATION? IF YOUR JOB INVOLVES ROUTINE
NUDITY, RUBBER SHOES, BLACK FISHNETS, OR A FRIGHT
WIG, YOU ALREADY KNOW ALCONE. THEY STOCK VISORA
BRAND   FOUNDATIONS   BY   CHRISTIAN   DIOR,   IF
YOU NEED TO LOOK PERFECT ON CAMERA, OR NICOTINE
STAINS   FOR   YOUR   TEETH   IF   YOU   DON'T.
IF YOU WANT TO ALARM YOUR BOYFRIEND, HOW ABOUT SOME
FAKE   BLOOD   OR   A   NEW   NOSE?
TRY FASTLASH, THE VERY BLACKEST MASCARA,
BE SURE TO STOCK UP ON MOLES AND
THOSE EYELASH CURLERS FROM
J A P A N .

henry street chamber **opera**
is opera on a **human,**
intimate, but **powerful scale.**
henry street **settlement**
466 grand **street**
call 279 4200 **for tickets**

lucky's
juice
joint 75
w. houston st.
388 0300

THE HAITIAN CABDRIVER COLD REMEDY

TAKE 12 LIMES. CUT THEM INTO QUARTERS. PUT IN SAUCEPAN AND ADD NYC TAP WATER TO COVER. BRING TO BOIL, THEN SIMMER UNTIL LIMES ARE TOTALLY MUSHY. ADD ENOUGH SUGAR TO MAKE THE THING DRINKABLE, AND SIMMER SOME MORE TIL IT'S A SYRUP. STRAIN AND DRINK IT AS HOT AS YOU CAN STAND IT.

wolf
paper
and
TWINE

680 sixth avenue

75 4870

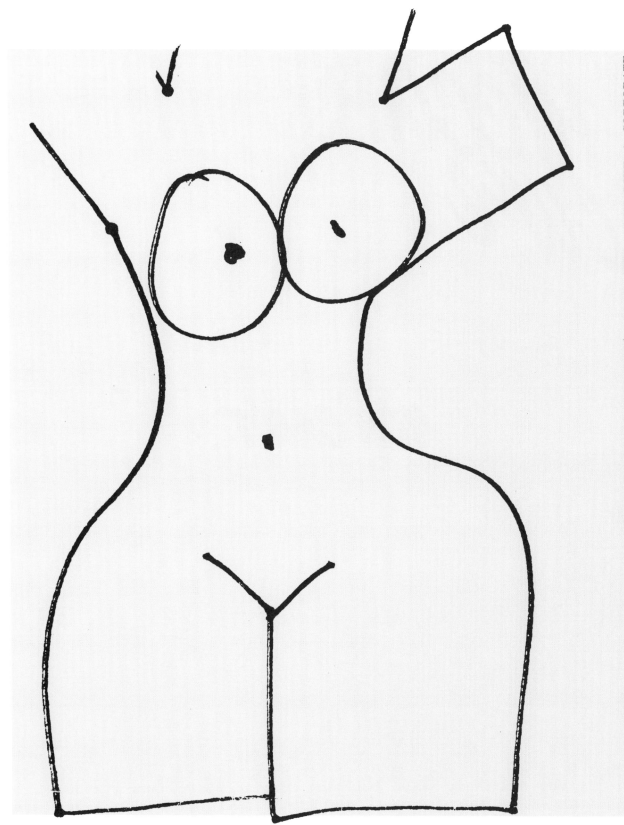

FOR REAL BODIES: SEXY CLOTHES IN NICE BIG SIZES THAT DON'T MAKE YOU LOOK LIKE A CORPORATE OUTER SPACE NUN. ASHLEY STEWART 166 CHURCH STREET 349 2520 OR 216 WEST 125 STREET 531 0800

the performance anxiety

HICCUP CURE

© 2003 laurie rosenwald

GUARANTEED TO WORK

ask somebody to say the following, very seriously, while staring deeply and hypnotically into your eyes:

HICCUP NOW! I'LL GIVE YOU 50 BUCKS!
DO IT! DO IT NOW!
WELL, WHAT ARE YOU WAITING FOR?
DO IT! DO IT NOW! etc. **YOU CAN'T.**

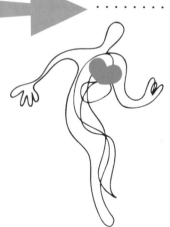

one day a friend of mine went to a party on the upper west side. guess who she met there. **isaac bashevis singer!** upon being introduced, *he put his hand on her leg* and asked, *"WHO DO YOU LIVE WITH AND WHO DO YOU LOVE?"* so much better than "what do you do?" who cares? this is the important stuff.

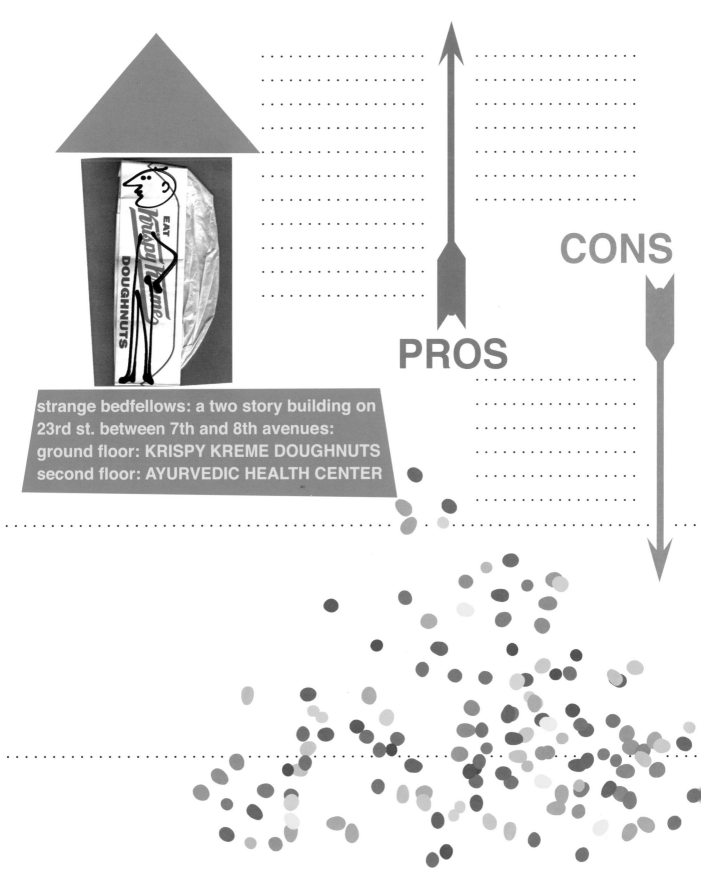

PROS

CONS

strange bedfellows: a two story building on
23rd st. between 7th and 8th avenues:
ground floor: KRISPY KREME DOUGHNUTS
second floor: AYURVEDIC HEALTH CENTER

how to be a native new yorker (OR AT LEAST NOT LOOK LIKE A TOURIST)

DON'T CALL 6TH AVENUE THE AVENUE OF THE AMERICAS.

DON'T PAUSE at THE top OF AN ESCALATOR.

IT's PRONOUNCED HOWSTON, NOT HOUSTON.

IF YOU STARE UP AT THE BUILDINGS AND YELL "C'MON GUYS!" TO YOUR GANG, WE'LL KNOW YOU'RE FROM KANSAS.

IF YOU WEAR A PECULIAR WOOLY ETHNIC HAT, WE'LL KNOW YOU'RE FROM VERMONT.

IF YOU ROUTINELY USE THE EXPRESSIONS "EXCELLENT", "AMAZING", OR "TOTALLY", WE'LL KNOW YOU'RE FROM AMERICA.

IF YOU WEAR A FANNY PACK, WELL, JUST DON'T.

IF YOU STROLL LEISURELY DOWN THE SIDEWALK WE'LL KNOW YOU'RE FROM SPAIN OR ITALY.

if you weave all over the sidewalk, don't. this is known as "continental drift."

AND DON'T

WALK THREE ABREAST.
DRESS LIKE YOUR FRIENDS.
PERM YOUR HAIR.
WEAR LITTLE GOLD JEWELRY WITH DIAMOND CHIPS IN IT.
STOP SUDDENLY ON THE STREET.
GO OUT ON FRIDAY OR SATURDAY NIGHT.
HANG AROUND MIDTOWN.
WEAR RUNNING SHOES WITH JEANS.
TRAVEL IN PACKS.
BUY ANYTHING ON CANAL STREET.
GO TO ANY RESTAURANT WITH INITIALS IN THE NAME.
TAKE BUSES.
DRIVE A CAR.

 and by the way.  buy designer perfume on canal street. remember it's just as authentic as it was the day it was bottled in 1998.

if you wouldn't want to be a member of a club that would have you as a member then you are already a native **new yorker.**

pearl paint co   308 canal st.   431 7932

the best art supply store anywhere, ever.

* GIFTS

It's not the Thought, it's the Thing.

DESIGN GEWGAWS AND GIFTS WITH REAL POWER!

125 GREENWICH AVENUE

989 4300

AT MXYPLYZYK

235 ELIZABETH STREET

334 9728

AT DAILY 235

YOU'LL FIND SMALL GIFTS FOR TASTEFUL WEIRDOS

do you speak
bespoke?

all my sharpest
gallery friends
get their suits
made there; when you
walk in you see an
autographed picture
of herve villechaise.
need i say more?
Mr. Tony 120 West 37th St.
telephone: 594-0930

the museum of tel

the freezing place
on a hot summer day
25 west 52 st.
621 6800

spend it watching
Pennies From Heaven
and The Singing Detective
by Dennis Potter

a great innovator.

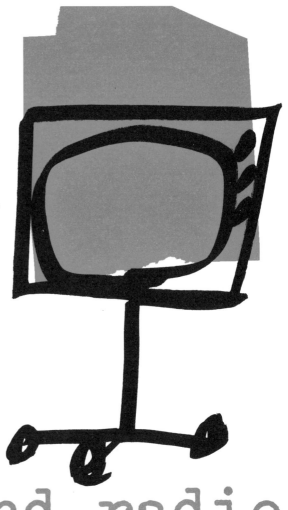

evision and radio

The Carlyle

MADISON AVENUE AT 76TH STREET
NEW YORK, N. Y. 10021

THE BEMELMANS BAR. LUDWIG BEMELMANS, CREATOR OF
"MADELINE" PAINTED THE WONDERFUL MURALS. MADISON AVE. AT 76TH STREET. 744 1600.
THE CARLYLE'S COOL, BECAUSE THERE'S NO "HOTEL LOBBY" SCENE. AND WHEN I GOT MARRIED THEY GAVE
US THE "NANCY REAGAN" SUITE FOR THE PRICE OF A REGULAR ROOM. THERE WAS A PIANO IN IT.

mary had
a little lamb
its fleece was
white as snow
she took it
down to pittsburgh.
and now look
at the damn thing.

*midnight express
custom valet*

keep your woolies white! free pickup and delivery, day and   night. jumpsuits $9.95.

alpana bawa

**BRILLIANT COLORFUL ORIGINAL UNUSUAL CLOTHES
THAT DON'T LOOK LIKE ANYONE ELSE'S   41 GRAND ST. 431 6367**
AREN'T YOU TIRED OF BLACK?

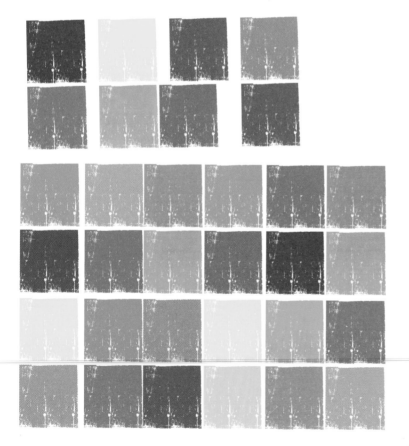

THE ROSENWORLD REPORT

some people watch the
weather channel, but you can't
improve on the jacket, sweater,
and t-shirt alert:

look out the window and see what they're wearing.

do
you read
"metropolitan
diary" in the
"times?" it's my
favorite section.
i remember a
story about
some
out-of-towners
babysitting their
grandson.
when they ran
out of milk, the
grandparents
asked where the
family usually
shopped, and
were surprised
when the boy
left the room and
came back with
binoculars.
he then got a
chair, put it by
the window,
climbed up, and
focused on the
awning
of a deli across
the street,
saying,
**"see that
phone
number? if you
call it, they
bring milk."**

A REAL NEW YORKER ·········

Better
Take a
Jacket!!

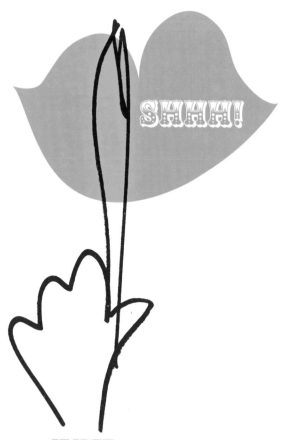

SHHH!

SECRET PLACES WITH NO SIGNS OR ANYTHING

THE VODKA BAR
AT THE ROYALTON HOTEL
JUST GO IN
AND SWERVE RIGHT.
44 WEST 44TH STREET

ORCHARD BAR
200 ORCHARD STREET
DARK, HIP AND
FUNKY MUSIC

CHUMLEY'S
86 BEDFORD STREET
ANCIENT, LITERARY,
BEERY

THE CAMPBELL APARTMENT
VANDERBILT ENTRANCE
GRAND CENTRAL STATION
TAKE THE ELEVATOR UP

read "The Bottom of the Harbor"
by Joseph Mitchell and

"The City in the Sea"
by A.J. Liebling. Because
New York is one.

staten island   south
ferry   ferry

wall street
ferry

fulton
ferry

trinity
church

schermerhorn
row

western union
telegraph building

st. paul's
chapel

shot
tower

post
office

say no to noise call 1888 677

beep blip bip bip beee honk bip bip nhe blonk
eee honk bip bip nhe blonk wray
blonk aaaahnk
wray honk bip bip nhe
nhheee aanhheee aaa
aa nn wraaa ooo weeaa
nhheee ooo waaaaah
waaaaooo waaaaah

I can't believe
that car alarms are legal.
why is their stuff worth
more than
my peace of mind?

I WAS 35 BEFORE I FOUND OUT ABOUT THE SECRET CONSERVATORY GARDEN. ENTER CENTRAL PARK AT 104TH STREET AND FIFTH AVENUE. QUIETUDE AND FORMAL BEAUTY.

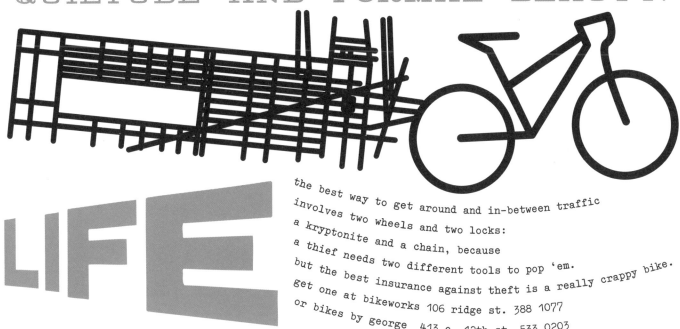

LIFE

the best way to get around and in-between traffic
involves two wheels and two locks:
a kryptonite and a chain, because
a thief needs two different tools to pop 'em.
but the best insurance against theft is a really crappy bike.
get one at bikeworks 106 ridge st. 388 1077
or bikes by george 413 e. 12th st. 533 0203

in the movie **the desk set,** katharine hepburn plays a new york public library reference

librarian. people simply call her up and ask any question at all and she answers it. just like that! like, **what are the four streets in new york spelled with only three letters?*** i found out this wonderful service still exists! when i called i started to mention **the desk set** but before i could get the words out she said, **yes, i'm katharine hepburn.** here is that number:

340 0849

or you can contact: ask@nypl.org and they'll e-mail your answer back to you!

the new york public library telephone reference service

* ANN street, DEY street, GAY street, and JAY street.

NEBRASKA'S LEGENDARY
WARRIOR RABBIT

learn swinging laughter, pigeon laughter, lion laughter, subway laughter, and high five laughter in your new "laughing yoga" class! i kid you not. laughing lotus   55 christopher street   414 2903

untitled has the kind of books and postcards you like if you like this book. 159 prince street   982 2088

hair

fancy shmancy
cuts and colors for
like thirty or forty
bucks instead of 200.
ask about
training nights at:

Louis Licari Salon
693 5th Ave.
517 8084

John Sahag
425 Madison Ave.
750 7772
call on Mondays

Frederic Fekkai
15 East 57th St.
753 9500

little tony's
for a "regular" haircut.
103 w. 11 st. 242 8028.
my father's barber's name is **"gus librizzi.**"

i feel this is the right name for a barber.

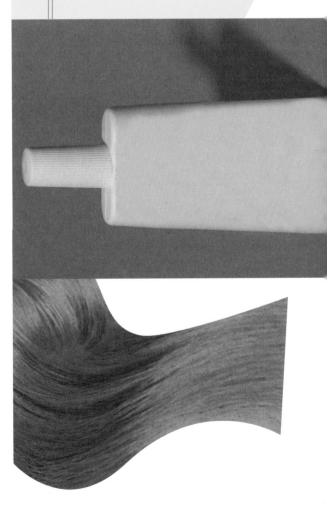

NYABINGHI

african gift shop

111 chambers st.
566 3336

my default setting is :

bar pitti

268 sixth ave.
between
bleecker and
houston
982 3300

try rigatoni pitti

KOOKY new york siGns

theres a store

then theres THAT THING painted on the side of a building NEAR CHURCH STREET

there's a funeral home
on 14th street between 8th and 9th avenues
called HOME FOR "FUNERALS"
it's the quotation marks
that make it all worthwhile.

a mystery   wrapped in

WHY DOES EVERY DELI
HAVE A TINY HANDWRITTEN SIGN
ON THE DOOR THAT SAYS:
～WE HAVE OATMEAL!～
IS IT SOME KIND OF CONTRABAND?

i love the series

on the corner of seventh avenue and 14th^{street} called bagelry. doesn't that sound like something you could get arrested for? grand bagelry.

AND WALKER STREET THAT SAYS LOOK FOR THE CLOTHESPIN TAG! THERE'S PIZZA PLUS PLUS ON CANAL STREET.

an enigma.

THE PHARMACY WITHIN

a sign at
yonah schimmel knishery
137 east houston street:
all orders **TO GO** must be
TAKEN OUT

GANGS OF NEW YORK

by herbert asbury

BILL THE BUTCHER

IF YOU THINK IT'S A VIOLENT WORLD OUT THERE
TAKE A LOOK BACK A HUNDRED AND FIFTY YEARS. IT WAS EVER THUS.
NO, IT WAS MUCH WORSE. AT LEAST WE HAVE PENICILLIN.

cherry
185 orchard street
358 7131

lucille's
antique center
27 west 26 st
691 1041

VINTAGE

pucci, if you're lucky

you know what?
i hate art. i mean "new" art. i like design.
these chelsea bums can't draw, so
they have to come up with gimmicks, or "controversial"
subjects and upsetting, repulsive materials.
then the critics have a lot to say, and the
museums buy into it. it's the emperor's new clothes.
but what's there to say about art that people understand?
what's there to say about a matisse? just look at it!
of course design can be expensive
and pretentious too.
but at least you can sit on it.

where
hip chinese
make the
congee scene:
sweet n' tart
restaurant
for the best blood
soup and the finest
snow frog jelly in town.
20 mott street. 964 0380

string, king, zeppelin, penguin, eggplant, breadfruit,
yankees, iceland, drain, betelgeuse, connecticut, glacier,
callas, weegee, ramones. whatever you
desire, the picture collection at the mid-manhattan
public library has a manila folder around it.
40th street and fifth avenue. 340 0878.

makes you glad you live here.

NOT A BROADWAY SHOW.......... this !

free
MEDITATION INSTRUCTION

AT THE
NEW YORK
SHAMBHALA CENTER
118 WEST 22 STREET
675 6544

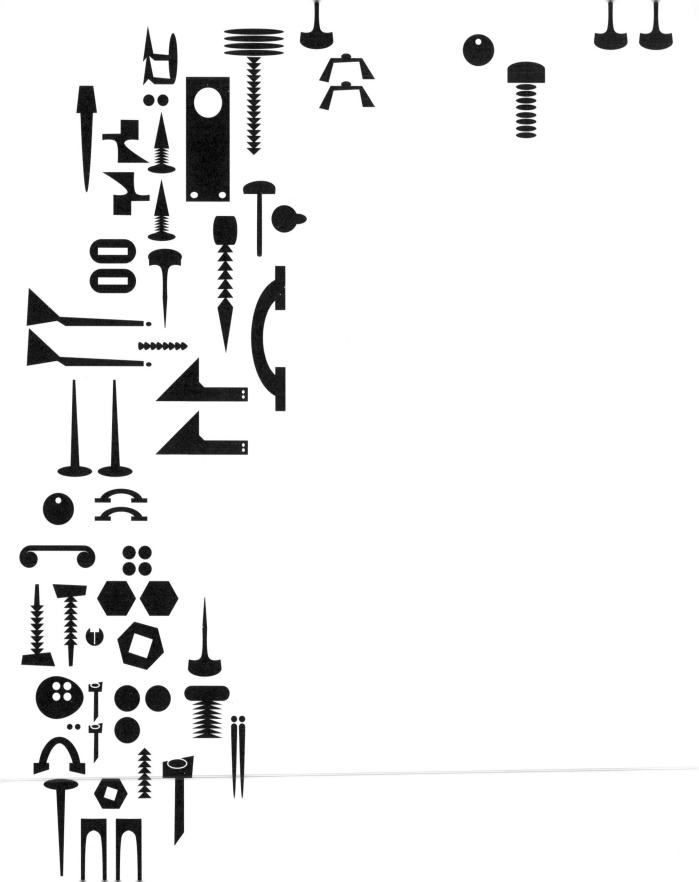

THE WILDEST
SELECTION OF KNOBS
& HANDLES IS AT
SIMON'S HARDWARE
421 THIRD AVE.
532 9220

Chandrika

BRIGHT GREEN SUPER-HERBAL
CHANDRIKA SOAP PUTS AVEDA TO SHAME.
$1.25 AT SPICE HOUSE, 99 1ST AVENUE
OR GO AROUND LEXINGTON AVENUE
FROM 24TH TO 28TH STREETS
TO STOCK UP ON MARMITE, CHUTNEY, AND KOHL.
OR BUY A LOVELY SAREE AT OM SAREE PALACE,
134 EAST 27TH STREET. 532 5620

POLITICALLY CORRECT PET ADOPTION

MAKE SURE EVERY PET
HAS A HOME.
THE FUND FOR ANIMALS
HAVE A HEART CLINIC
NEUTERS PETS FOR FREE.
355 WEST 52 ST.
977 6877

WWW.CITYCRITTERS.ORG AND
WWW.PETFINDER.ORG
CITY CRITTERS RESCUES
NEW YORK ANIMALS IN TROUBLE
INFO@CITYCRITTERS.ORG

CAT

ISE AND SHINE!
A-1 WAKE UP SERVICE
233 3399

back where i came from by a.j. liebling

time and again by jack finney

* up in the old hotel by joseph mitchell

eloise by kay thompson

2 great small bookstores:

gotham book mart
41 w. 47 st. 719 4448

gryphon books + records
2246 broadway at 81 st. 362 0706

*this one is a must. the best new york stories of all time.
'in winter i'm a buddhist, and in summer i'm a nudist.' – joe gould
(from "joe gould's secret"
by joseph mitchell.
this book is included in "up in the old hotel.")

BOOK

Bereket
Kebab
House 187
E. Houston St.
475 7700
Cafeteria 119
7th Ave. 414
1717
Munson Diner 600
W. 49th St. 246
0964
Corner Deli 106
Kenmare St. 925 9360
Market Diner 572
Eleventh Ave. 695 0415
Woo Chon (korean) 8-10 W.
36th St. 695 0676

OPEN aLL night

THE MULTI-PORK SANDWICH

NOT ONE, NOT TWO,

BUT **3** KINDS OF **PORK.**

THIS TEENY SHOP SERVES SCRUMPTIOUS SANDWICHES ON PERFECT FRENCH BREAD FOR ABOUT 3 BUCKS.

VIET- NAM BANH MI SO 1   369 BROOME ST. 219 8341

café gitane

where smoking is not merely tolerated. it is MANDATORY.
242 matt st. 334 9552

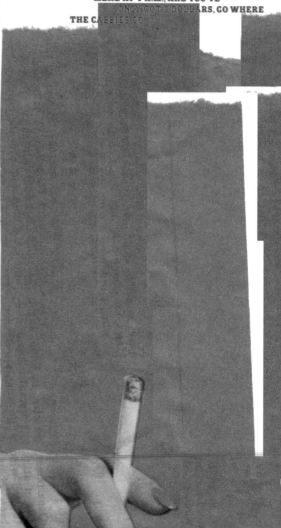

CALL
WHEN NATURE
PUN

WHEN YOU ABSOLUTELY,
POSITIVELY HAVE TO
HAVE A COMPLETE VEGETARIAN
MEAL AT 4 A.M., AND YOU'VE
ONLY GOT 3 DOLLARS, GO WHERE
THE CABBIES GO

INGATURE

CALLS YOU

JABI

114 EAST 1ST STREET

OR,

my favorite phone booth
is in the corner of grange hall
uptown
i like the ones restaurant
at the russian tea room 50 commerce st.
150 west 57th st. go to your
don't use those non-verizon phones. immediate right just inside
you'll be sorry.
the
plaza hotel
768 5th ave.
has great phones and
bathrooms
from 5th ave. entrance
also, in the saloon bar next to go to left of palm court
the oyster bar in grand central and past eloise's portrait
there's a ladies room with and gift shop
giant leather armchairs that
look like hands and a "lips" sofa from the '60s.

madame romaine de lyon

132 east 61 st.
758 2422

bizarre omelette
specialist

if you enjoy vodka-scented embarrassment,
belly dancing, schmaltz, and chopped liver, you'll love
Sammy's. 157 Chrystie St. 673 0330
a food critic once advised "bring your cardiologist"

Sammy's
roumanian steak house

I ❤ NY.

NEW YORK CITY

If You live
in new york,
even if
you're catholic,
you're jewish
-lenny bruce

The Carmine Street Irregulars, aka The New York Jugglers **have been in existence for over a decade.** Originally started by Bill Wachspress and Brian Dube, the group has evolved into an eclectic and revolving **bunch with some meets drawing over 50 jugglers.** All levels of expertise are represented from the 3 bag novices to the 5 club experts on unicycles. So learn to juggle! *Check the website for details and directions.*

http://ntscomputer.com/mystere/csi/index.html

Carnegie DELICATESSEN RESTAURANT

York
TURDAY, DECEMBER 13, 1997

GLADIATOR'S GYM

DO THE HUSTLE!
OR THE SALSA.
SANDRA CAMERON
TEACHES IT ALL.
(the merengue is super easy)
199 LAFAYETTE STREET   674 0505

*ie test
a friend does
mischief
if he makes
a sieve of your
handkerchief
*but
neither weird sheik
seizes leisure either

iq test

contact
the testing coordinator
greater new york mensa
cloty@juno.com

PORGY

crab

Tuna

SaLMON

RAZoR ClaM

catfishBLUEfish

gulf SHRimp

snapper

FRESHER AND CHEAPER
IN CHINATOWN

TAN MY MY
249 GRAND ST. 966 7878

NEW HAI CANG
71 MULBERRY ST. 385 0981

ted meuhling

makes the world's prettiest, purest earrings.
47 greene st. 431 3825

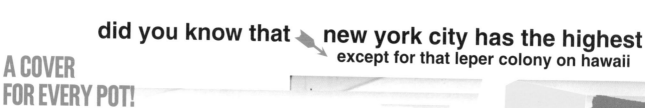

did you know that ➘ **new york city has the highest**
except for that leper colony on hawaii

A COVER
FOR EVERY POT!

do you appreciate nature and
photography and sports and music
and food that is not bad? do you enjoy
being entertained
by entertainment? do you have
the patience of a saint,
the hands of a surgeon, and a heart
you could pour on a waffle?
are you highly educated, well-read,
bright and creative, yet down to earth?
comfortable in plus-fours, serape
and burnoose? i'll believe that once
you've seen me in a ballgown.
then we'll both have a good laugh.
are we agreed? splendid! let us
then repair to a secluded, yet
reassuringly public rendezvous and
enjoy nervously together
the pleasures of overpriced caffeine.

www.timeoutny.com/personals

density of single people on earth?

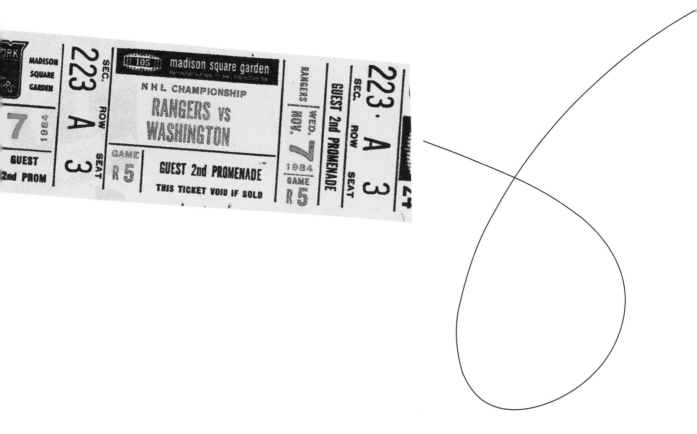

HELICOPTER TOURS!
liberty helicopters

967 2099

THE WHISPERING WALL
IN GRAND CENTRAL

THE GRAND CENTRAL OYSTER BAR AND RESTAURANT
GRAND CENTRAL TERMINAL * LOWER LEVEL

order oyster pan roast.
PAN ROAST. not chowder. trust me.

what is it? nobody knows. but it's the sexiest dish in town.
incidentally, not so long ago, staten island had the
best oyster beds in america.

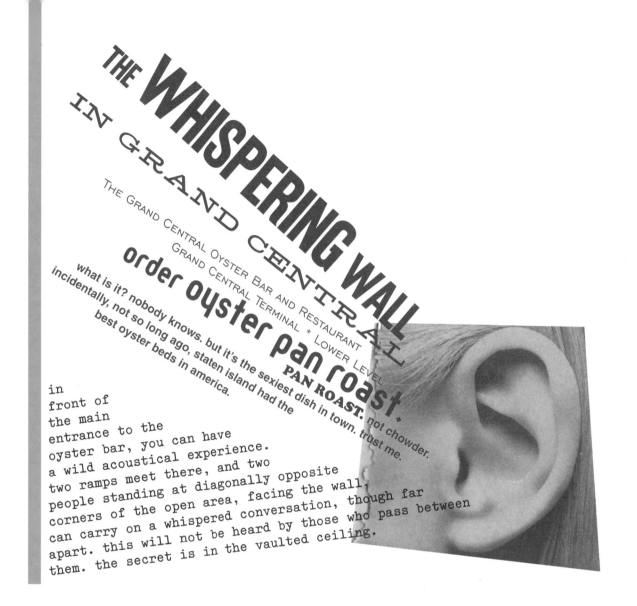

in
front of
the main
entrance to the
oyster bar, you can have
a wild acoustical experience.
two ramps meet there, and two
people standing at diagonally opposite
corners of the open area, facing the wall,
can carry on a whispered conversation, though far
apart. this will not be heard by those who pass between
them. the secret is in the vaulted ceiling.

SUBWAY

my favorite new york show is **subway Q & A.**
it's **voyeurism, democracy,**
and friendliness in guerilla action. a camera crew
jumps into a subway car and asks total
strangers what they're cooking for dinner, inviting
the stranger sitting next to them over.
they arrange dates for singles in the car, and
ask people what was the worst lie they ever told.
they took a group of strangers over to
one guy's apartment, bought mops and buckets,
and cleaned it all up. then they ordered a pizza.
they got one couple married in the subway,
and held a subway olympics. metro tv subway Q+A.
check local listings

OI, VAI!

Attention Goyim; Don't be farblondzhet! This little guide really comes in handy when you don't want to look like a nishtikeit, a shmo, a shmendrik, or a shlemiel. **Besides, we need two words for "enema."**

A biseleh • A very little

A broch! • Oh hell! Damn it!! A curse!!!

A broch tsu dir! • A curse on you!

A farshlepteh krenk • A chronic ailment

A feier zol im trefen • He should burn up!

A glick hot dir getrofen! • Big deal! Sarcastic.

A klog tzu meineh somin! • A curse on my enemies!

A leben ahf dir! • You should live!

A mentsh on glik is a toyter mensh • An unlucky person is a dead person.

A metsieh fun a ganef • It's a steal

A nishtikeit! • A nobody!

A shandeh un a charpeh • A shame and a disgrace

Ahf mir gezogt! • I wish it could be said about me!

Ahzes ponim • Impudent fellow

Aidel • Cultured or finicky

Alevei! • It should happen to me (to you)!

Alter Kucker • A lecherous old man

An alteh machashaifeh • An old witch

An alter trombenick • An old bum

Arumgeflickt! • Plucked! Milked!

Arumloifer • Street urchin; person who runs around

Az a yor ahf mir. • I should have such good luck.

Az och un vai! • Touch luck! Too bad! Misfortune!

Azoy? • Really?

Azoy gait es! • That's how it goes!

Azoy gich? • So soon?

Azoy vert dos kichel tzekrochen! • That's how the cookie crumbles!

Baitsim • Testicles

Baren (taboo) • Fornicate: bother, annoy

Baroygis • Angry, petulant

Bashert • Fated or pre-destined

Bobkes • Small things, triflings, peanuts, nothing

Borsht circuit • Hotels in the Catskill Mountains

Bris • Circumcision

Bubee • Friendly term for anybody you like

Chamoyer du ainer! • You blockhead! You dope!

Chap a gang! • Beat it!

Chosid • Rabid fan

Chropen • Snore

Chutzpeh • Brazenness, gall, baitzim

Cristiyah • Enema

Dershtikt zolstu veren! • You should choke on it!

Drai mir nit kain kop! • Don't bother me!

Draikop • Scatterbrain

Drek • Human dung, feces, insincere talk

Druchus • The sticks (way out in the wild)

Ech • A groam, a disparaging exclamation

Ei! Ei! • Yiddish exclamation equivalent "Oh!"

Einhoreh • The evil eye

Es brent mir ahfen hartz. • I have a heartburn.

Es macht mir nit oys. • It doesn't matter to me.

Es tut mir a groisseh hanoeh! • It gives me great pleasure!(often said sarcastically

Es vet gornit helfen! • Nothing will help!!

Faigelah • Bird (also used as a deragatory reference to a gay person).

Farblondzhet • Lost, bewildered, confused

Farblujet • Bending your ear

Fardrai zich dem kop! • Go drive yourself crazy!

Farfoylt • Mildewed, rotten, decayed

Farkuckt (taboo) • Dungy, shitty

Farmatert • Tired

Farmisht • Befuddled

Farmutshet • Worn out, fatigued, exhausted

Farshlepteh krenk • Fruitless, endless matter

Farshnoshket • Loaded, drunk

Farshtunken • Smells bad, stinks

Farshvitst • sweaty

Feinkochen • Omelet, scrambled eggs

Feinshmeker • Hi falutin'

Finster un glitshik • Miserable

Foiler • Lazy man

Folg mich! • Obey me!

Fonfen • Speak through the nose

Fortz • Fart

Frassk • Slap in the face

Fressen • Eat like a pig, devour

Funfeh • Speaker's fluff, error

Gai avek! • Go away

Gai in drerd arein! • Go to hell!

Gai kucken ahfen yam! • Get lost

Gai platz! • Go split your guts!

Gai shlog dein kup en vant! • Go bang your head against the wall

Gai strasheh di vantzen • You don't frighten me! (Lit., Go threaten the bed-bugs)

Gai tren zich. (taboo) • Go fuck yourself

Ganef • Crook, thief, burglar, swindler, racketeer

Gantseh megilleh • Big deal! (derisive)

Gantser k'nacker! • Big shot!

Gatkes • Long winter underwear

Gebrenteh tsores • Utter misery

Geharget zolstu veren! • Drop dead!

Gelaimter • Person who drops whatever he touches

Gembeh! • Big mouth!

Genug iz genug. • Enough is enough!

Geshtroft • Cursed, accursed; punished

Gevaldikeh Zach! • A terrible thing! (often ironically)

Gezunteh moid! • Brunhilde, a big healthy dame

Gib mir nit kain einorah! • Don't give me a canary! (Americanism, Lit., Don't give me an evil eye)

Gotteniu! • Oh G-d! (anguished cry)

Goy • Any person who is not Jewish

Goyim • Group of non-Jewish persons

Greps • Blech; a burp if it's a mild one

Grob • Coarse, crude, profane, rough, rude

Grois-halter • Show-off, conceited person

Groisseh gedilleh! • Big deal! (said sarcastically)

Groisser gornisht • Big good-for-nothing

Groisser potz! (taboo) • Big penis! Big prick! (deragatory or sarcastic)

Hak mir nit in kop! • Stop bending my ear

Handlen • To bargain; to do business

Hartsvaitik • Heart ache

Heizel • Whorehouse

Hekdish • Decrepit place, a slumhouse, poorhouse; a mess

Hikevater • Stammerer

Hinten • Rear, rear parts, backside, buttocks

Hit zich! • Look out!

Hitsik • Hothead

Hoizer gaier • Beggar

Holishkes • Stuffed cabbage

Host du bie mir an avleh! • So I made a mistake. So what!

Ich bin dich nit mekaneh • I don't envy you

Ich feif oif dir! • I despise you! Go to the devil! (Lit., I whistle on you!)

Ich hob dir! • Drop dead! Go flap you ears!

Ich hob dich in bod! • To hell with you!

Ich vel dir geben kadoches! • I'll give you nothing!

Kabaret forshtelung • Floorshow

Kalamutneh • Dreary, gloomy, troubled

Kalyeh • Bad, wrong, spoiled

Kam vos er kricht • Barely able to creep

Kam vos er lebt • He's hardly (barely) alive.

Kamtsoness • To be miserly

Kaneh • An enema

Karger • Miser, tightwad

Kasokeh • Cross-eyed

Kibbitzer • Meddlesome spectator

(A) Kitsel • Tickle

Klainer gornisht • Little prig (Lit., A little nothing)

Klipeh • Gabby woman, shrew, a female demon

(A) Klog iz mir! • Woe is me!

Klop • Bang, a real hard punch or wallop

Klotz (klutz) • Ungraceful, awkward, clumsy person

Klotz kasheh • Foolish question

K'nish (taboo) • Vagina

K'nishes • Baked dumplings

Kochleffel • One who stirs up trouble

Kolboynik • Rascally know-it-all

Krechtser • Blues singer, a moaner

Kuck im on (taboo) • Defecate on him!

Kuck zich oys! (taboo) • Go take a shit for yourself!

Kuk im on! • Look at him!

Kurveh • Whore

Kush in toches arein! (taboo) • Kiss my behind!

Kushinyerkeh • Cheapskate; woman who comes to a store and asks for a five cents' worth of vinegar in her own bottle

K'vetsh • Whine, complain; whiner

Leiden • To suffer

Lemeshkeh • Milquetoast, bungler

Lig in drerd! • Get lost! Drop dead!

och in kop • Hole in the head.

Lokshen • Noodles

Loz mich tzu ru! • Leave me alone!

Makeh • Plague, wound, boil, curse

Manzer • Bastard, disliked person, untrustworthy

Mashugga • Crazy

Me ken brechen! • You can vomit from this!

Me lost nit leben! • They don't let you live!

Mein cheies gait oys! • I'm dying for it!

Meshpucha • Extended family

Meshugass • Madness, insanity, craze

Meshugeh ahf toit! • Crazy as a loon. Really crazy!

Mieskeit • Ugly thing or person.

Moisheh kapoyer • Mr. Upside-Down! A person who does everything backwards

Mosser • Squealer

Moyel • Person who performs circumcisions.

Muttelmessig •
Meddlesome person, kibitzer

Na! • Here! Take it. There you have it.

Nafkeh • Prostitute

Nafkeh bay-is •
Whorehouse

Nar ainer! • You fool, you!

Nebach • It's a pity. Unlucky, pitiable person.

Nebbish • A nobody, simpleton, weakling

Nem zich a vaneh! • Go take a bath!

Nisht gefonfit! • Don't hedge. Don't fool around.

Nisht getrofen! • So I guessed wrong!

Nisht gut • Not good, lousy, bad.

Nisht do gedacht! — It shouldn't happen! G-d forbid! (Lit., May we be saved from it! [sad event]

Nishtikeit! • A nobody!

Nishtu gedacht! • It shouldn't happen! G-d

forbid!

Nit kain farshloffener • A lively person

Nochshlepper • Hanger-on, unwanted follower

Nosh • Snack

Nu? • So? Well?

Nudnik • Pesky nagger, nuisance, a bore

Nudje • Annoying person, badgerer

Och un vai! • Alas and alack: woe be to it!

Oi, a shkandal! • Oh, what a scandal!

Oi, Vai! • Dear me! Expression of dismay or hurt

Oi vai iz mir! • Woe is me!

Oisgeshtrobelt! •
Overdressed woman.

Ois•shteler • Braggart

Oiver botel •
Absentminded: getting senile

Olreitnik! • Nouveau riche!

Ongeblozzener • Stuffed shirt

Ongepatshket • Cluttered, disordered, scribbled, sloppy, muddled, overly-done

Ongetrunken • Drunk

Ongetshepter •
Bothersome hanger-on

Onzaltsen • Giving you the business; bribe

Opgeflickt! • Done in! Suckered! Milked!

Opgekrochen • Shoddy

Opgelozen(er) • Careless dresser

Opgenart • Cheated, fooled

Opnarer • Trickster, shady operator

Opnarerei • Deception

Oremkeit • Poverty

Oych mir a leben! • This you call a living?

Oyfen himmel a yarid! • Much ado about nothing! Impossible! (Lit., In heaven there's a big fair!)

Oysgedart • Skinny, emaciated

Oysgematert • Tired out, worn out

Oysgemutshet • Worked to death, tired out

Oysvurf • Outcast, bad person

Paigeren zol er! • He should drop dead!

Parshiveh • Mean, cheap

Patteren tseit • To lounge around; waste time

Petseleh • Little penis

Phooey! fooey, pfui • disbelief, distaste, contempt

Pipek • Navel, belly button

Pishechtz • Urine

Pisher • Male infant, a little squirt, a nobody

Pisk-Malocheh • Big talker-little doer!

Pitshetsh • Chronic complainer

Pitsvinik • Little nothing

Plagen • Work hard, sweat out a job, suffer

Plagen zich • To suffer

Plats! • Burst! Bust your guts out! Split your guts!!

Plyotkenitzeh • A gossip

Preplen • To mutter, mumble

Prietzteh • Princess; finicky girl; (having airs, giving airs; being snooty) prima donna!

Prost • Coarse, common, vulgar

Prostaches • Low class people

Prostak • Ignorant boor, coarse person, vulgar man

Prosteh leit • Simple people, common people; vulgar, ignorant, "low class" people

Proster mentsh • Vulgar man, common man

Ptsha • Cows feet in jelly

Pupik • Navel, belly button, gizzard, chicken stomachs

Pupiklech • Dish of chicken gizzards

Se brent nit! • Don't get excited! (Lit., It's not on fire!)

Se shtinkt! • It stinks!

Shaigitz • Non-Jewish boy; wild Jewish boy

Shaineh maidel • pretty girl

Shat, shat! Hust! • Quiet! Don't get excited

Shatnes • Proscription

against wearing clothes that are mixed of wool and linen

Shikker • Drunkard

Shikseh • Non-Jewish girl

Shkapeh • A hag, a mare; worthless

Shkotz • Berating term for mischievous Jewish boy

Shlang • Snake, serpent; a troublesome wife; penis

Shlecht veib • Shrew (Lit., a bad wife)

Shlemiel • Clumsy bunglar, an inept person

Shlep • Drag, carry or haul

Shlimazel • Luckless person. Unlucky person; one with perpetual bad luck (it is said that the shlemiel spills the soup on the shlimazel!)

Shlog zich kop in vant. • Break your own head!

Shlog zich mit Got arum! • Go fight City Hall!

Shlub • A jerk; a foolish, stupid or unknowing person, second rate, inferior.

Shlump • Careless dresser, untidy person

Shlumperdik • Unkempt, sloppy

Shmaltzy • Sentimental, corny

Shmatteh • Rag, anything worthless

Shmegegi • Buffoon, idiot, fool

Shmeichel • To butter up

Schmeikel • To swindle, con, fast-talk.

Shmendrik • nincompoop; an inept or indifferent person; same as shlemiel

Shmo(e) • Naive person, easy to deceive; a goof

Shmok (taboo) • Self-made fool; obscene for penis: derisive term for a man

Shmulky! • A sad sack!

Shmuts • Dirt, slime

Shnook • A patsy, a sucker, a sap, easy-going, person easy to impose upon, gullible

Shnorrer • A beggar who makes pretensions to respectability; sponger, a

parasite

Shoyn genug! • That's enough!

Shreklecheh zach • A terrible thing

Shtik drek (taboo) • Piece of shit; shit-head

(A) Shtunk • A guy who doesn't smell too good

Shtup • Push, shove; vulgarism for sexual intercourse

Shtup es in toches! (taboo) • Shove (or stick) it up your rectum (ass)!

Tandaitneh • Inferior

Tararam • Big noise, big deal

Tateh-mameh, papamama • Parents

Temp • Dolt

Temper kop • Dullard

Traif • Forbidden food, impure, contrary to the Jewish dietary laws, non-kosher

Trombenik • A bum, no-good person, ne'er-do-well

Tsaddik • Pious, righteous person

Tsedrait • Nutty, crazy

Tsedraiter kop • Bungler

Tsemisht • Confused, befuddled, mixed-up

Tshepen • To annoy, irk, plague, bother, attack

Tu mir nit kain toives. • Don't do me any favors.

Tumler • A noise-maker (person); an agitator

Tut vai dos harts • Heartbroken

Tzufil! • Too much! Too costly!

Yachneh • A coarse, loud-mouthed woman;

Yenems • Someone else's; (the brand of cigarettes moochers smoke!)

Yenteh • Gabby, talkative woman

Yentzen (taboo) • To fornicate, to whore

Yukel • Buffoon

HERE'S A NEW YORK STORY: THERE'S A TINY RESTAURANT IN THE WEST VILLAGE WHICH SERVES AT LEAST FIVE HUNDRED KINDS OF SOUP. THE OWNERS HAVE FIVE CHILDREN. THEY'RE A BIT HARD TO KEEP TRACK OF ALL THE TIME. SO ONE DAY THE MOTHER COULDN'T FIND THE BABY, WHO WAS ABOUT ONE AND A HALF. SHE FRANTICALLY SEARCHED THE RESTAURANT AND THEN OUTSIDE. SHE SAW NOBODY, BUT SHE HEARD A NOISE COMING FROM THE BLUE NEW YORK TIMES VENDING MACHINE ON THE CORNER. OF COURSE HER BABY WAS INSIDE IT. SHE HAD TO PAY THE 7 5 CENTS TO GET HIM OUT, BUT IT WAS WELL WORTH IT.

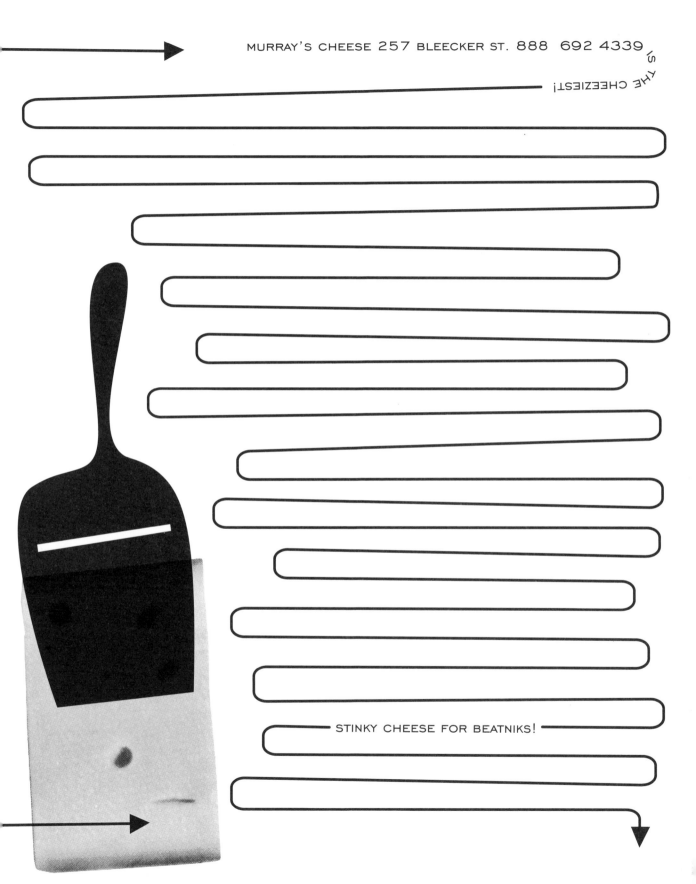

MURRAY'S CHEESE 257 BLEECKER ST. 888 692 4339 IS THE CHEEZIEST!

STINKY CHEESE FOR BEATNIKS!

a
NEW
YORK
Wino
is a
happy
wino!

WOW! WINE ON SUNDAY. NOW THAT'S A BRILLIANT IDEA. WOW! WINE ON SUNDAY. NOW THAT'S A BRILLIANT IDEA.WOW! WINE ON SUNDAY. NOW THAT'S A BRILLIANT IDEA. OH! WINE ON SUNDAY. NOW THAT'S A BRILLIANT IDEA. WOW! WINE ON SUNDAY. NOW THAT'S A BRILLIANT IDEA. WOW! WINE ON SUNDAY. NOW THAT'S A BRILLIANT IDEA.VINTAGE NEW YORK, ON THE CORNER OF BROOME AND WOOSTER STREETS IN SOHO, HAS MORE THAN 100 FROM NEW YORK STATE, SO THEY FOUND SOME CRAZY LOOPHOLE THAT LET'S THEM SELL WINE ON SUNDAY! ALL THE WINES THEY CARRY CAN BE TASTED ON THE PREMISES. IT IS THE ONLY WINE STORE IN THE CITY ALLOWED TO OPEN ON SUNDAY. VINTAGE NEW YORK IS AT 482 BROOME ST. AND THE PHONE NUMBER? 226 9463

HE BAGEL

OR stop by at midnight at one of
kossar's bialys
367 grand st
473 4810
AND GET A HOT
ONE

RESTAURANT

170 w 4 st
255 0106

the best non-power breakfast
in town.

the **real** ones are at
ess·a·bAgEL
359 first avenue 260 2252

super tacky
bulgarian nightclub
mehanata
416 broadway
625 0981   have a pilsner urquell
great dj

THIS IS A PLACE WHERE A LOVELY PIANIST PLAYS A WHITE PIANO ON AN ARTIFICIAL ROCK UP NEAR THE CEILING WHILE YOU EAT BULGOGI HANSUNG GARDEN RESTAURANT

563 1285

42 W. 35 ST.

THE REALISTIC NEW YORK DIET

WHAT WEIGHT WATCHERS WILL NEVER UNDERSTAND ABOUT REAL LIFE SO I HAD TO INVENT

EVERY DAY BREAKFAST AT HOME:
ENORMOUS BOWL OF OATMEAL
WITH "SKIM PLUS" BRAND MILK,
WALNUTS, APPLES,
DRIED CRANBERRIES
OR ANY FRUIT. CINNAMON OR VANILLA.
NEW YORK TIMES
CROSSWORD AND
ESPRESSO.

LUNCH AT A JAPANESE PLACE:
BENTO BOX SPECIAL.
EITHER SASHIMI OR SOME KIND OF
TERIYAKI OR NEGIMAKI.
SALAD AND OSHITASHI.
NO RICE. TEA.

DINNER AT TOMOE OR JAPONICA
OR TASTE OF TOKYO OR HASAKI

LUNCH AT A KOREAN PLACE:
BULGOGI AND KIMCHEE.
TEA. NO RICE.

HEY, IT WORKS FOR ME!

LUNCH AT A COFFEE SHOP:
GRILLED CHICKEN SOUVLAKI SANDWICH.
IT COMES WITH RAW VEGETABLES AND TZAZIKI YOGURT SAUCE.
FEED THE PITA BREAD TO SOME PIGEONS. ICED TEA.
NO SWEET N' LOW. IT'S POISON.

OR ANY JAPANESE PLACE:
EDAMAME. GREEN SALAD AND HIJIKI, OSHITASHI OR SEAWEED SALAD,
AS MUCH AS YOU WANT. UNLIMITED SASHIMI OR COOKED FISH.
NO RICE. AND AS MUCH SAKE
OR WINE AS YOU LIKE.

DINNER AT BAR PITTI OR ANY ITALIAN PLACE:
SAUTEED SPINACH. BEAN SALAD WITH TUNA,
OR MAYBE THE LIVER. NO BREAD. NO SPAGHETTI!
HALF A BOTTLE
OF RED WINE. ESPRESSO.

SNACK: APPLE, ALTOIDS, PISTACHIOS.

LE DINER AT PASTIS OU PRUNE OU
L'ACAJOU OU ODEON OU LE ZINC OR
ANY CONTINENTAL OR **FRENCHY** TYPE OF PLACE:
A BIG HUNK OF LAMB. HARICOTS VERTS.
PAS DE GRATIN DAUPHINOIS! PAS DE FROMAGE! AT PASTIS, TRY
THE GRILLED SARDINES ON TOAST WITHOUT THE TOAST.
UN BOUTIELLE DE MERLOT.

LUNCH AT A VIETNAMESE PLACE:
VIETNAMESE COLD BEEF SALAD
OR SHRIMP AND
PAPAYA SALAD OR BOTH.
NO RICE. TEA.

nells
246 west 14 street.
a real nightclub with good music. part of it's quiet and comfy,
and part of it's loud and dancy.

ONE GREAT NIGHTCLUB FOR SALSASOULAFROCUBANBRAZILIAN MUSIC AND DANCING IS
S.O.B.'s. 204 VARICK STREET. ASK ANYBODY. 243 4940

stash (my friend liza's friend)
has this store for
sneakomaniacs
called NORT 235
(tron, backwards)
with the kind of sneakers
you won't find at niketown, man.
235 eldridge street. 777 6102

another sneakoholic mecca is
ALIFE RIVINGTON CLUB
158 rivington street.   375 8128

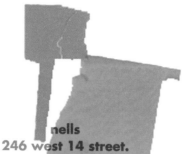

CENTURY 21
22 CORTLAND STREET 227 9092
BARGAIN BASEMENT MISSONI & MOSCHINO
FOR MISS THING!

SELF SERV

at broadway and walker street,
is without question my favorite new york store.
among other things, they carry grapefruit juice,
light bulbs, 5 dollar suitcases, party hats,
votive candles, salad spinners, rit dye, murphy's oil soap,
translucent aprons, bon-ami cleanser,
lu brand biscuits, potting soil, woks, lobster steamers,
aspirin, shelf paper, applesauce, duct tape,
ironing board covers, "for rent" signs,
oilcloth, alarm clocks, reese's peanut butter cups, steel wool,
noisemakers, clothespins, toilet paper at four for a dollar,
garbage cans, drill bits, shampoo, pistachio nuts,
and little friskies with labels in russian.

RANDEAS / RANDOM (background watermark text)

210 east 9th street. 473 3327

a story about HASAKI: one night madonna shows up
and as usual there's a long line. they don't take
reservations. she goes to the front with her friends
and says "do you know who i am?" and they **H A S A K I**
say, "of course, you're madonna!
get in line." and to her credit, she did.

J A P A N E S E   R E S T A U R A N T S
the utterly italian restaurant with a very very japanese chef and a totally japanese staff. basta pasta **37 west 17th street.**
the pasta is oddly shiny and a little bit too organized. quattrocento goes bento. but very good.
T H A T   A R E   I T A L I A N 366 0888

union square
farmers market
schedule: mon., wed., fri., sat. 8AM-6PM (5PM during winter)

FILL IN THE BLANKS

rabble rouser

EveRymaN

nogoodnik

alibi

GURU

DOES WINDOWS

CASH COW

sugar daddy

PEOPLE TO THANK WHEN YOU GET AN OSCAR

raison d'etre

confidant

OFFSPRING

SCAPEGOAT

poor relation

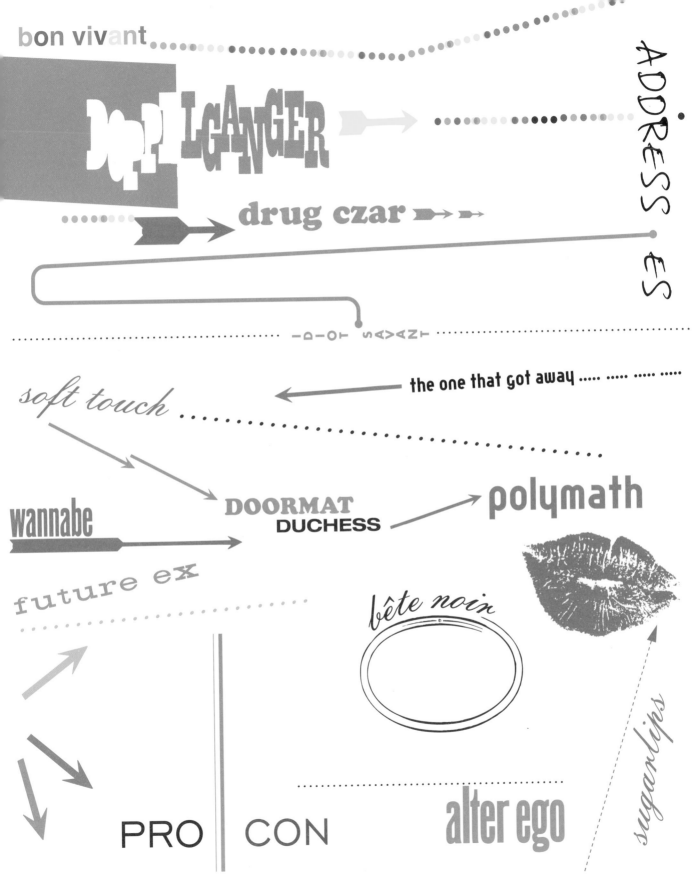

bon vivant

DOPPELGANGER

ADDRESSES

drug czar

IDIOT SAVANT

the one that got away

soft touch

polymath

wannabe

DOORMAT
DUCHESS

future ex

bête noir

sugarlips

PRO | CON

alter ego

name

notes

telephone home

telephone work

telephone somewhere else

regular mail

e-mail

something else

whatever

WHO?	PHONE	AT WORK	PHONE SOMEPLACE ELSE	E-MAIL	REGULAR MAIL	whatever

WHO?

PHONE

AT WORK

PHONE SOMEPLACE ELSE

E-MAIL

REGULAR MAIL

PEOPLE I KNOW

WHO?

PHONE

AT WORK

SOMEPLACE ELSE

E-MAIL

REGULAR MAIL

WHO?

PHONE

AT WORK

SOMEPLACE ELSE

E-MAIL

REGULAR MAIL

WHO?

PHONE

AT WORK

PHONE SOMEPLACE ELSE

E-MAIL

REGULAR MAIL

SOMEPLACE ELSE

AT WORK

E-MAIL

REGULAR MAIL

WHATEVER

WHO?

PHONE

AT WORK

PHONE SOMEPLACE ELSE

E-MAIL

REGULAR MAIL

WHO?

PHONE

PHONE AT WORK

PHONE SOMEPLACE ELSE

E-MAIL

REGULAR MAIL

1 --

2 --

3 --

4 --

5 --

6 --

7 --

8 --

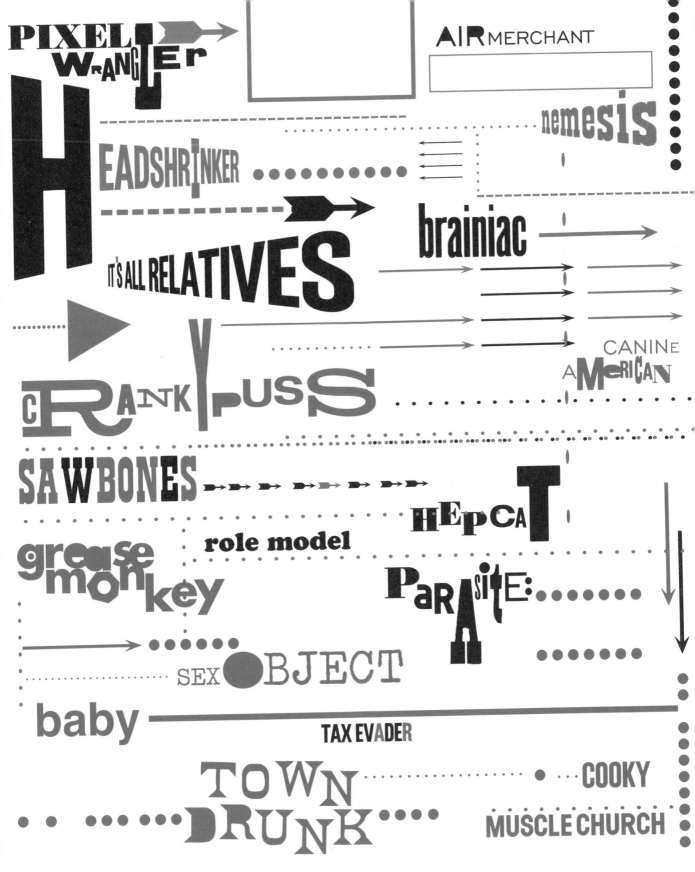

gramercy park: desirable, historical, a bit dull. read "time and again."

murray hill: the most boring, residential.

west village: avoid bleecker and eighth streets around sixth avenue or macdougal. the far west parts near hudson and greenwich streets are the loveliest. gay!

east village: gritty, younger, ukranian, bars. little india.

upper east side: dog walkers, nannies, cashmere poncho ladies who lunch, money, museums, good doctors.

central park: great "summerstage" concerts, and the great lawn really is great. there are falcons in the park! it's fun to watch the broadway show league baseball games. so beautiful. the best.

flatiron: silicon alley. graphic designers and photographers and the hipper ad agencies and some good stores, like paul smith. and weiss & mahoney.

upper west side: shrinks, actors, dancers, singers, gay and straight families. well-adjusted, residential. fairway is the best supermarket in town.

midtown: west side: tourists, showbiz. east side: all business, posh shopping. but 57th street is good. still some traditional galleries. ninth avenue in the 40s has good food markets.

west 30s (garment district) is the absolute worst. avoid. 32nd street is koreatown–great food!

soho: avoid on weekends. boutiques, mostly. broadway is proletariat shopping.

tribeca: celebrities at bubby's. loft buildings, no big deal.

chelsea: lovely residential streets in the west 20s. pretentious galleries with great door handles, fantastic light fixtures, window shades and paint jobs. the emperor's new clothes.

meat packing district: the newer soho, still some meat!

nolita: converted garages with 500 dollar 80's redux by young designers with a trust fund. i hope. some good small restaurants.

below chambers street; business again. unhip. stressful.

lower east side: orchard street, ludlow street. interesting hispanic/jewish/young hipster mix. bars and nightspots. some bargains. good brassieres. the east part of chinatown is exotic and weird.

harlem: i don't know harlem well enough, honestly. but the gospel services are great.

BIASED
UNFAIR
NEIGHBORHOOD
RUNDOWN